HOW TO DRAW BIRDS, FISH AND REPTILES

How to Draw
BIRDS,
FISH *and*
REPTILES

by Arthur Zaidenberg

Abelard-Schuman
New York

Printed in the United States of America

L.C. Card 62-9069
ISBN 0-200-71812-6 RB

5   6   7   8   9   10

CONTENTS

BASIC DRAWING MATERIALS

Some of these drawings were made with a very soft pencil. Others were made with an ordinary pen, and still others with a fine, pointing water-color brush and India ink.

Several of the drawings in India ink were made on scratch board. It may be bought at most artist supply shops.

Scratch board is an illustration paper covered with a thin layer of hard smooth plaster.

When you draw ink lines or large flat black areas, you may scratch the surface through the black exposing the white paper underneath. Very pretty effects may be achieved in this method of drawing, and corrections may be made in your ink lines with a simple scraper knife. Any pocketknife will do.

Remember, however, that the important thing is to draw, draw and draw. Any tools—your school pencils and pens, your crayons or school chalks—are ready to help you make good drawings.

Carry a sketch pad with you whenever you go out and draw everything that interests you.

INTRODUCTION

When I was an art student in Paris many years ago, there was a great teacher of drawing who was also a great actor. He did not give his performances on the stage, but in our classroom. He would send us into roars of laughter with his antics, but he was serious—and he taught us an important principle of drawing through his acting.

The principle he taught was this: if you wish to draw any object or living thing well, you must imagine that you *are* that thing. You must *feel* and try to *be* like the thing you draw.

If you are about to draw a bird, you must "act out" in your mind and with your drawing strokes, the *nature* of a bird. Lightness, speed, grace, and flight must fill your mind and guide your hand.

If you draw a rock, you must become heavy and hard and your hand must convey that feeling.

Our teacher would take on the facial characteristics of a bird or a rock or a fish, and it was very funny to watch, but his drawings had the character and spirit of a bird or a rock or a fish. Everyone who draws well follows that same procedure, although he may not do it in such an elaborate and amusing way as did my old teacher.

This book will teach methods of drawing birds, fish and reptiles.

Each of these creatures has many features known to you from having seen them in life and in pictures.

But do you know them? Have you met them?

You see your fellow students every day, but until you meet and know them personally you are strangers.

It is somewhat more difficult to get to know a bird or a fish, or especially a snake, but you must try to acquaint yourself with the special "birdlike" or "fishlike" or "snakelike" qualities so that your drawing will take on those qualities.

It is not difficult to draw, but it is not easy to draw a thing in such a way that the person who sees your drawing will *feel* what you felt when you did it, and understand the thing you drew as you understood it. That is *good* drawing, and it is art.

That is what this book will try to teach you to do.

There are thousands of different species of each of the creatures we will deal with here. We cannot hope to study more than the main characteristics of each group. If you learn to draw the flight character and the swim character and the stealthy crawl character of our subjects, you will begin to draw them well, and with practice and love, beautifully. You will get great pleasure out of such drawings, and so will those who see them.

BIRDS

The society of birds is enormous. There are giant birds too large and heavy to take off from the ground in flight, like the ostrich and the emu. There are birds so tiny and fast in their movements that they are almost impossible to follow with the eye—the hummingbird is such a creature.

There are great round fat birds and tall, slim ones. There are fierce, predatory, flesh-eating birds, and there are mild-mannered, seed-pecking birds. There are birds of gorgeous plumage, magnificent in shape and color, and there are drab, ugly birds.

The birds which concern us most in this book are the flying birds, because flight is the most characteristic quality of the species, and its special nature gives them great appeal as drawing subjects.

In these pages we will study the general structure of wings and the streamlined form of a bird's body, which enables it to leave the ground and soar into the air.

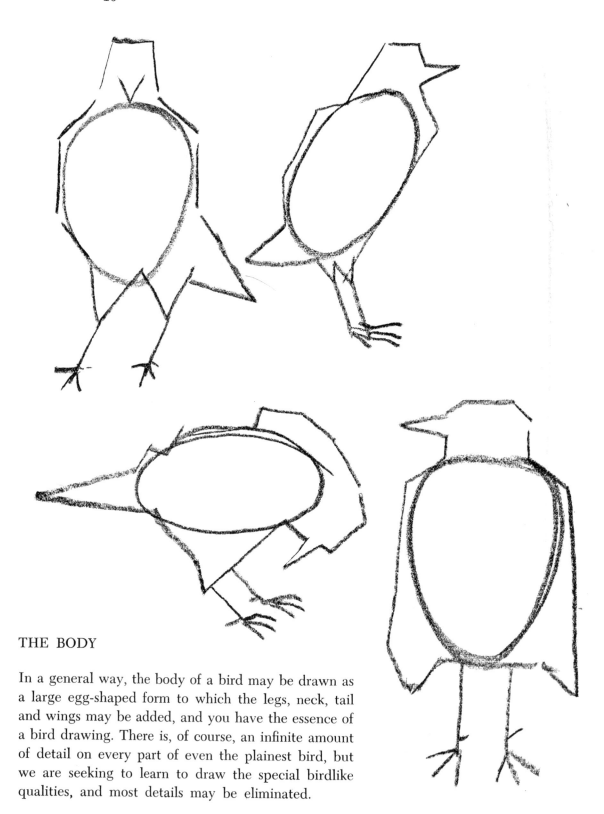

THE BODY

In a general way, the body of a bird may be drawn as
a large egg-shaped form to which the legs, neck, tail
and wings may be added, and you have the essence of
a bird drawing. There is, of course, an infinite amount
of detail on every part of even the plainest bird, but
we are seeking to learn to draw the special birdlike
qualities, and most details may be eliminated.

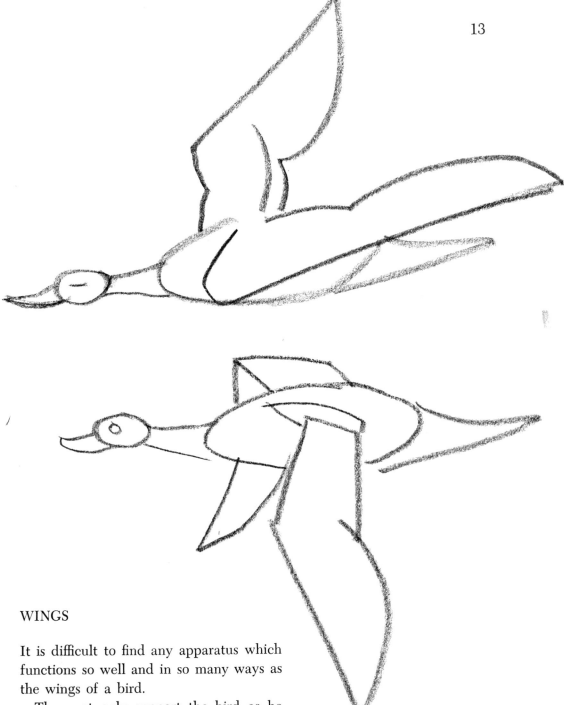

WINGS

It is difficult to find any apparatus which functions so well and in so many ways as the wings of a bird.

They not only support the bird as he soars in the air, they also propel him at tremendous speed. They act as brakes in the process of landing, and as balancers and stabilizers as he perches precariously on a swinging branch.

Birds use the soft warmth of wing feathers as shelter for their heads in sleep and protection for their young.

Many birds use their wings to beat their enemies in combat.

Their lightness and flexibility, as well as their surprising strength, allow for these varied uses.

Try to indicate those virtues in your drawings of wings.

The wings of a bird are exquisitely designed instruments for flying, and their flexible beauty is worth a good deal of study and drawing practice.

The broad spread and wide surface of wings, when fully extended, permit a bird to hover at almost a standstill before landing.

The streamlining in nature's design of birds,
a design which man has copied in airplanes
and missiles, allows for speed with the least
air resistance.

18

The fierce birds of prey, like the eagle, hawk, vulture and falcon, are equipped with wings of extra power and heavy, sharp claws. Their beaks are hooked for tearing the flesh of their prey.

Many water birds have webbed feet for paddling purposes.

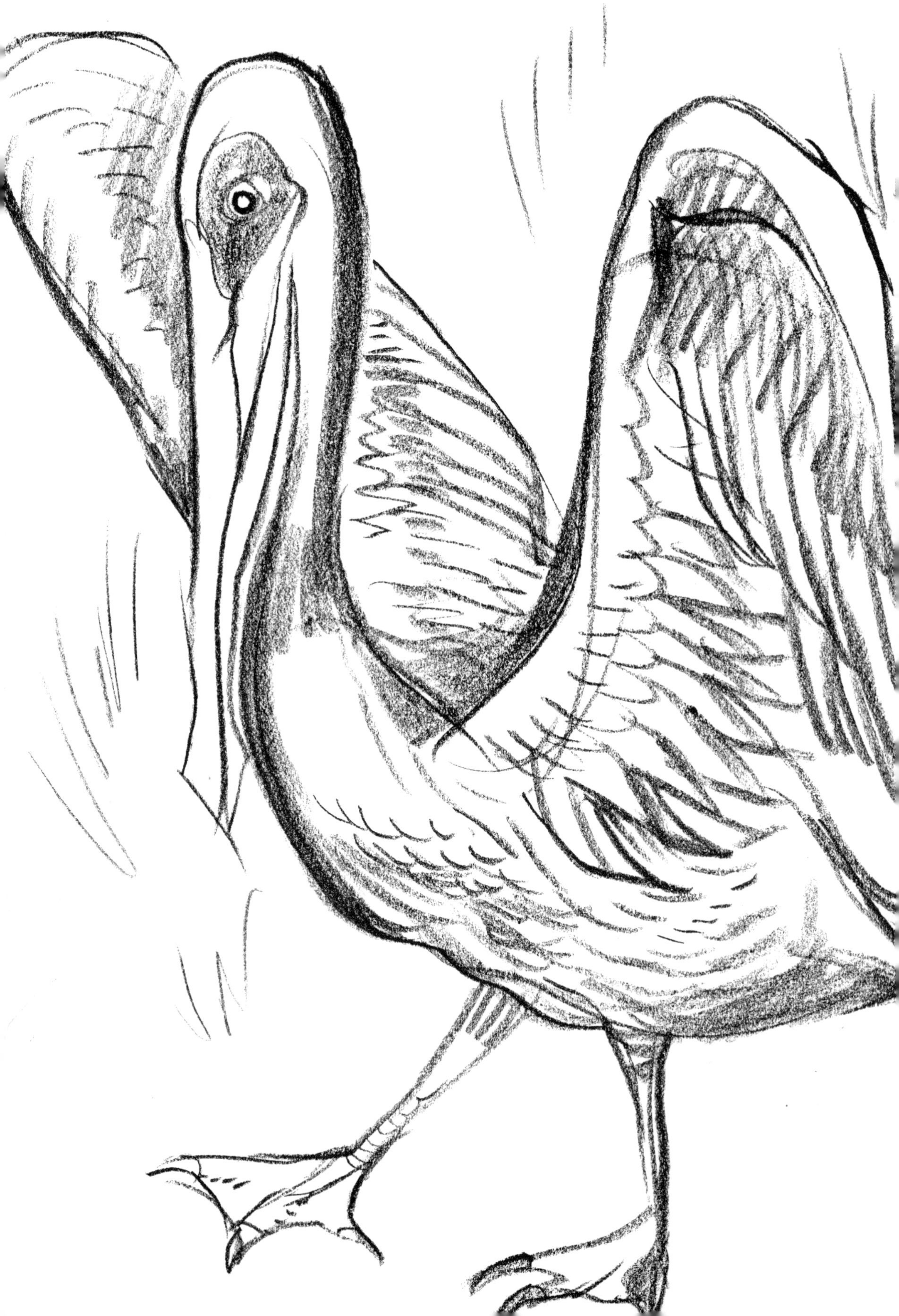

FISH

Fish are fascinating, beautiful creatures, hard to get to know intimately as one can most animals and even many reptiles. They never seem to notice us. They are, however, available for close observation in many places, public aquariums, home fish bowls and shallow ponds.

In fact, because they ignore humans so completely, one may observe their most intimate living habits more readily than most species. When people complain about not having enough privacy, they use the expression, "It's like living in a fish bowl."

Fish have backbones which make them "vertebrate" animals, but there ends their similarity to any other species of creature. They live entirely in water and breathe through gills. There are many thousands of species of fish, and we cannot hope to deal with more than a few of them in these pages.

We shall cover those whose shapes are most typical in each group.

Most are streamlined, but many are blunt and fat, others are long and slim as snakes, and some are shaped like flat pancakes. Their shapes, evolved through thousands of years of living in certain waters, depend on depth, temperature, currents and requirements for avoiding enemies.

Some fish are fierce and dangerous; most are mild and timid. Some live by eating other fish, and others by eating insects. Some are huge and others very, very tiny. All are interesting. Let's examine a few and try to draw them.

As in trying to learn to draw any object, drawing a fish demands a reduction of the complex details of the shimmering, scaly body to its basic, simple form. See how the divisions are made here. Four or five basic designs make up the parts of the body.

Those fierce, predatory tigers of the sea called sharks are full of sinuous grace as they rush through the waters.

Draw the sinister menace at the same time as you draw
their long beautiful lines.

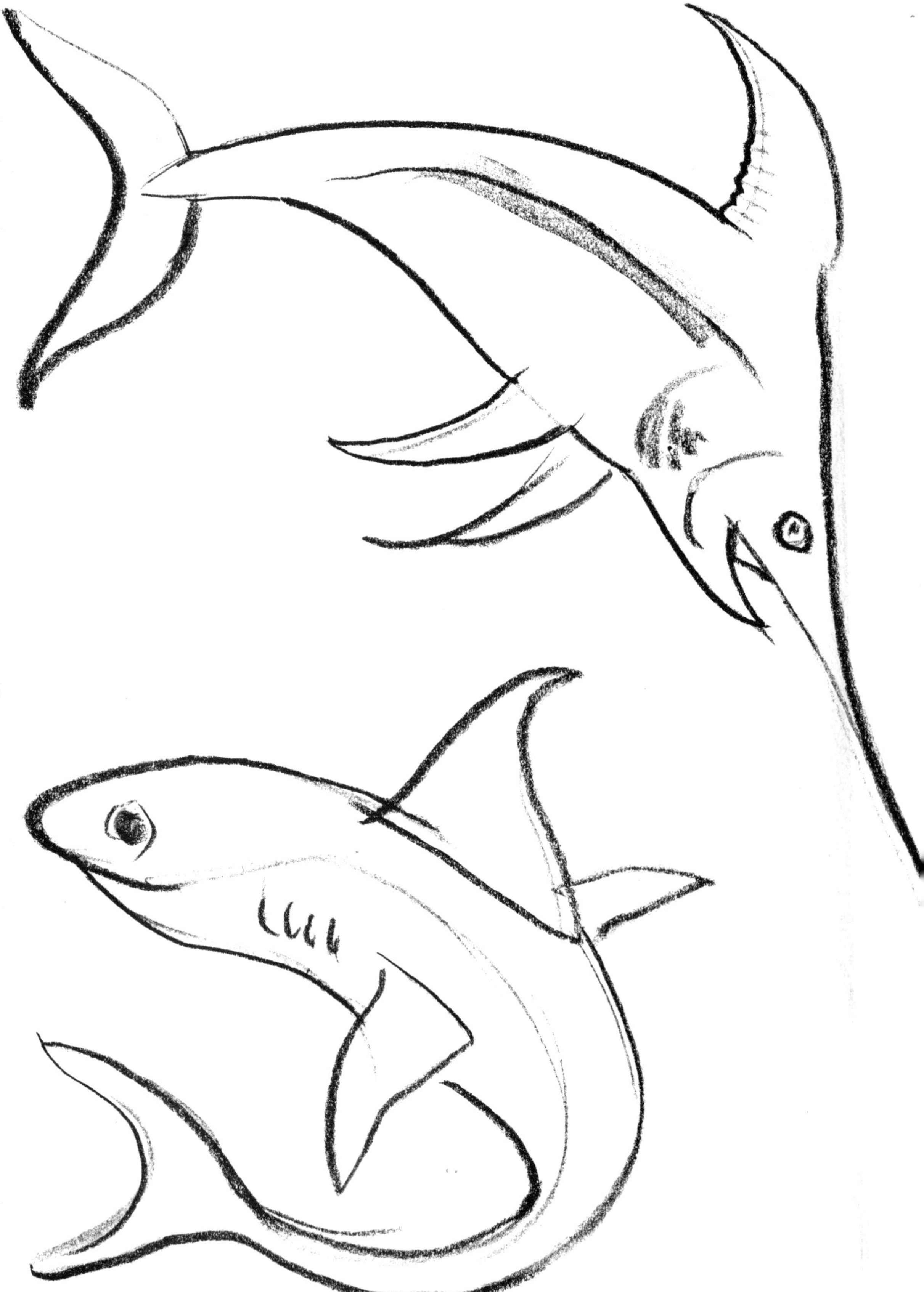

38

Inseparable from a good drawing of a live fish is the suggestion of its natural habitat, water.

There is no one way to draw the translucent flow of water. You must create a style of your own in expressing that sparkling fluid.

Very often a free "scribble" technique will give the effect you want.

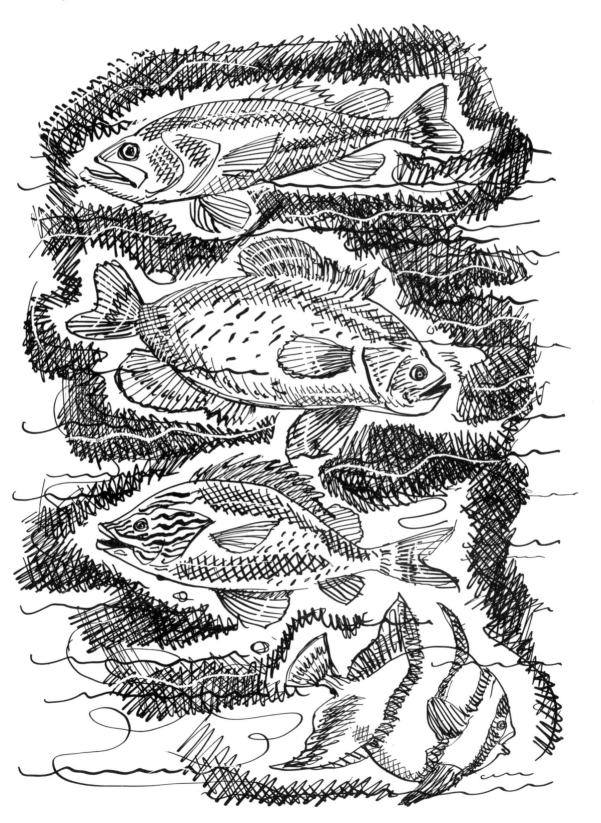

REPTILES

Reptiles are cold-blooded, air-breathing animals. They usually have scales or armor plate of some sort. They crawl on their bellies or waddle on short, crooked legs.

Except for snakes, reptiles have four legs. Most reptiles lay eggs which are covered with a kind of leathery skin. The types of reptiles fall into the following general groups, but many variations of each species exist.

1. Snakes: Scales all over their long bodies. No legs.
2. Turtles: They have short tails and four crooked scaly legs. The turtles have long, leathery necks which can be pulled into the hard shells carried on their backs.
3. Lizards: Small, fast-moving, four-legged, scaled animals.
4. Alligators: Enormous, lizard-like, huge-jawed animals with rows of sharp teeth.
5. Frogs and Toads: They are small, hopping and swimming creatures with powerful hind legs and short, dainty forelegs.
6. Prehistoric Reptiles: Many species. They are no longer in existence, but their appearance has been established from fossils and bones pieced together to give us an accurate picture of what they looked like millions of years ago.

Very few people love reptiles. There are many reasons for this lack of friendship between people and reptiles, some of which are not based on good grounds. Only a few snakes are poisonous, and many species of snakes make good pets and are useful in keeping down the rodent population.

Most turtles are harmless, and those whose snapping jaws are dangerous are very shy of humans and only too glad to be left alone.

Crocodiles and alligators are not exactly gentle creatures suitable as pets, but they, too, are shy of people, and if one doesn't choose them as swimming companions, they are easy to avoid.

Probably the main reason for the unpleasant feelings most people have towards reptiles is their unusual means of locomotion.

The slither of a snake along the ground, the weird crawl of the alligator or lizard, the heavy drag of the tortoise, make us feel uncomfortable.

If you wish to draw them well, it is this curious, characteristic means of covering ground that must be expressed in order to get their unique nature.

Of course, your drawing does not move. Having drawn it, it remains in one position on the paper. But you can "suggest" their strange action and thereby capture its character.

When you make your first series of drawings of snakes they will probably look like long, slender ropes.

But the snake is alive, and he has a long line of bones which, though flexible, also limits his movements.

A snake cannot bend sharply at right angles, like a thin rope.

Every movement of a snake is graceful, performed in long, rhythmic coiling and uncoiling.

Practice making flowing, curving lines to resemble the snake's movements.

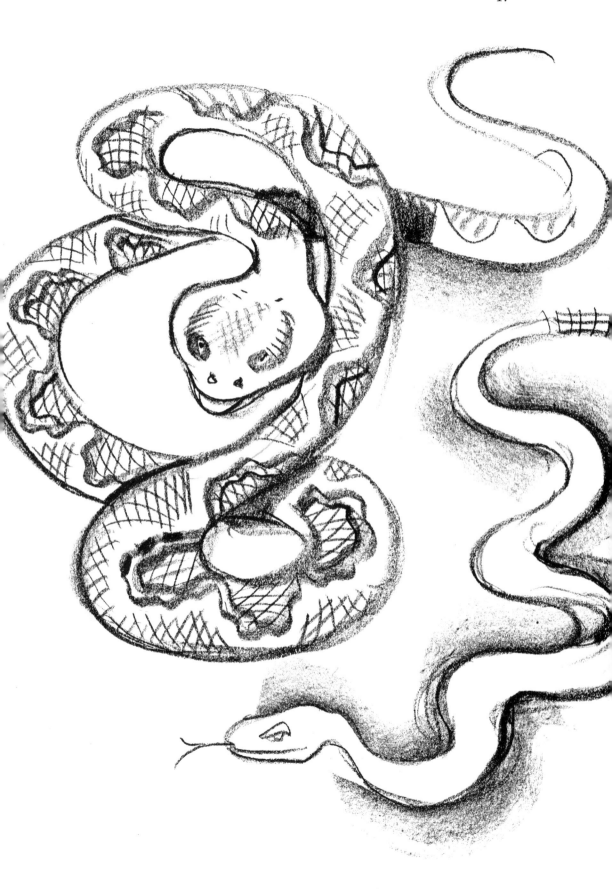

A snake can only raise his head and body close
to the head about one third of his entire length.
He cannot stand up on his tail section.

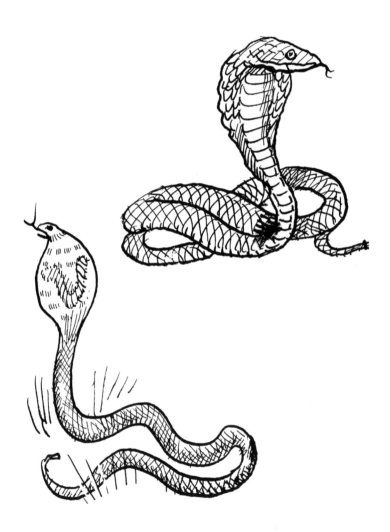

Don't try to draw all the scales and every inch of the design.

Actually, the designs on a snake's skin are intended by nature to "camouflage" or hide him from his enemies and from his prey. The patterns are partially hidden by the grass and leaves in which he moves. When a snake slithers along rocks or sleeps on a hot, flat stone, which he loves to do, his patterns are usually hidden more or less by the coiling and uncoiling.

Since we are more interested in drawing living animals than in dead specimens, the "lost and found" quality of the scale designs is important to preserve.

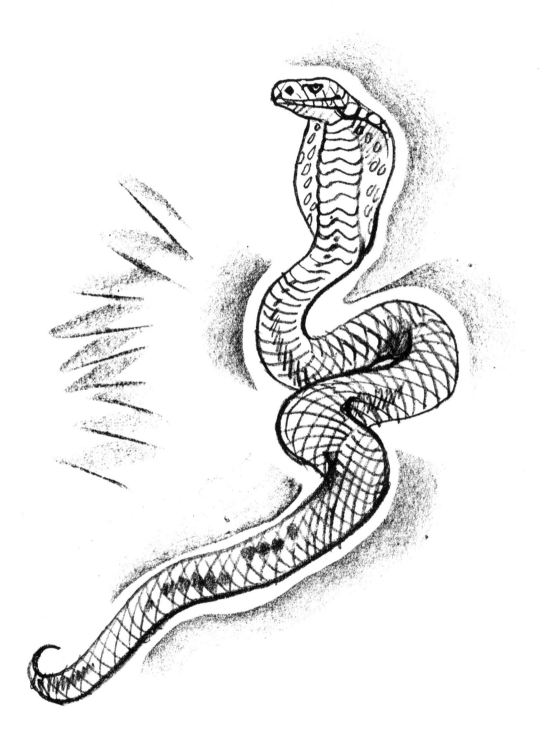

52

The large snapping turtles have small shells and heavy necks and large heads. Their legs are also very thick and strong. Their sharp beaks are dangerous, and the snap of their jaws breaks heavy sticks.

Some turtles have long, sharp nails on their feet; some species have flippers instead of feet. The latter are the sea-going turtles.

You won't see many horned lizards and Gila monsters, but they are interesting to draw and are like most lizards in their movements.